A HANDBOOK ON PARENTING GRANDCHILDREN

by:
Mary Ellen Davis

Gotham Books

30 N Gould St.
Ste. 20820, Sheridan, WY 82801
https://gothambooksinc.com/

Phone: 1 (307) 464-7800

© 2023 *Mary Ellen Davis*. All rights reserved.

No part of this book may be reproduced, stored in a retrieval system, or transmitted by any means without the written permission of the author.

Published by Gotham Books (December 19, 2023)

ISBN: 979-8-88775-801-5 (H)
ISBN: 979-8-88775-799-5 (P)
ISBN: 979-8-88775-800-8 (E)

Because of the dynamic nature of the Internet, any web addresses or links contained in this book may have changed since publication and may no longer be valid.

The views expressed in this work are solely those of the author and do not necessarily reflect the views of the publisher, and the publisher hereby disclaims any responsibility for them.

THE GRANDPARENTING JOURNEY:

LEADING THE WAY

Grandparenting is a fulltime, different, difficult, endeavor filled with love, ambivalence, wondering, questioning, pleasure, appreciation and excitement.

It is different because grandparents are different—older, wiser, and less energetic. The times are different and children are definitely different—so much younger, "wiser" (when compared to their parents at the same age), and more articulate and "all-knowing."

Grandparenting is difficult because of the energy consumption, the time, the work and the involvement in caring for and raising grandchildren today. The grandparenting job is filled with ambivalence because of the feelings of doubt about raising grandchildren. But, after considerable self-talk and unconditional acceptance of the fact that you and the grandchildren are a family, you begin detailing the map for the active journey.

Contents

Acknowledgements viii

Foreword ix

Dedication x

Chapter One: Beginning the Journey 1

    Behavior 2

    Family Adjustments 3

Chapter Two: Making Choices 5

    Teaching and Reinforcing Values 6

Chapter Three: Self-Direction 9

    High Self-Esteem/Self-Confidence 9

    Competence: 9

    Independence 10

    High Moral Character 10

    Being an Asset within the Group 10

    Internal Point of Control 11

    External Point of Control 11

Chapter Four: Health 12

    Grandparents' Physical and Mental Health. 14

Chapter Five: Education 15

    Life Skills 14

Chapter Six: School Involvement 19

Chapter Seven: Children's Home Library 21

    Home Transformation 22

Chapter Eight: Technology Kids 23

Chapter Nine: Religious And/Or Spiritual Guidance 25

    Family: Keeping in Touch 26

Chapter Ten: Social Activities 27

    Play Dates 27

    Family Gatherings 27

  Visitations.. 28

  Reunions 28

  Vacations 28

   Attending Various Museums, Theatres, Theme Parks............................... 30

Chapter Eleven: Youth Activities...31

Chapter Twelve: Family History 33

Chapter Thirteen: The Job 34

References 36

Acknowledgements

I extend wholehearted thanks to the following persons who allowed me to discuss the intent of this manual and to seek feedback on the content:

Alleen Ball, grandmother, for reading, offering assistance and making suggestions for content.

Mati Bates, retired business woman and grandmother for listening, giving valuable suggestions, discussing, reading and sharing her knowledge and wisdom.

Annie Curry, retired educator, for reading discussing content, intentions and offering feedback.

Janice Daniels, educator, administrator for reading and making suggestions for use in schools to assist grandparent caregivers.

James Taylor, retired middle school principal, and Priscilla Taylor (grandparents) for critical reading and offering literary suggestions.

Dr. Marcelett Henry (retired) California State Department of Education for reading and offering many meaningful suggestions.

Cristina Haley, elementary school teacher, for reading the draft document and providing corrections and suggestions.

Bessie McCollum, great-grandmother, for discussions sharing knowledge and many years of experience raising grandchildren.

Cassandra, Morgan, and Damien, the talented Grandchildren who provided the original illustrations.

Foreword

This book is not intended to be an advisory on the much-written-about subject of Grandparenting. It is sharing rather than telling. Its intent is to *share information* about raising grandchildren, to *remind grandparents* of the energy, dedication, and commitment involved in raising grandchildren and the necessity to engage in *preventive health* practices. It is meant to *share experiences* and to *support the efforts* of parenting grandchildren.

Dedication

I dedicate this book to my grandchildren—

Cassandra

Morgan

Damien

Charlie

Kwame

for whom I have endeavored to take the Grandparenting Journey.

chapter

ONE

BEGINNING THE JOURNEY

*We must nurture our children with confidence.
They can't make it if they are constantly told that they won't.*
- George Clements

Grandchildren are the conduit that build and retain memories of grandparents' childhood and youth, which keeps them grounded, focused and continually looking forward and planning ahead.

The joys and the challenges—sometimes almost synonymous and sometimes totally foreign to each other—garner love that's impossible to imagine, and engage one in a search for the physical and mental strength that leaves the body and mind absolutely conscious of the age and the endurance necessary to think 10 to 15 years hence. "According to the 2000 Census, more than 2.1 million children are being raised solely by grandparents or other relatives." *(Oregon State University Extension Family and Community Development. Internet 2009).* Raising grandchildren requires a general as well as a specific set of guidelines. Thinking about and preparing for grandchildren require a complete change of plans from retirement leisure, anytime vacations, cooking when and if one chooses, sleeping-in any morning beyond 7 a.m., (perhaps some weekends and holidays), stroll-shopping, talking on the phone with friends without having to stop and answer a list of continuous questions such as: "Is that your friend?" "May I have a popsicle or ice cream and peanut butter?" "Will you take us to the park?" "Let's play dress-up!" "Do you know how to play catch?" "May I play on the computer?"

Grandchildren living with grandparents are among an elite group of fast-growing households. A study by Rachel Pruchno and Dorothy McKenney published in *The Journal of Gerontology*, revealed that "The fastest growing types of households since 1990 are those which do not include either of the grandchildren's parents." (Internet: 2009)

Behavior. Too much or too little concern. While grandparents are conscious of showing too much or too little concern for grandchildren's behaviors—positive or negative—they struggle with the effort to make sure they provide total and proper care. They give individual grandchildren special attention based on need, unwavering love and behavior. Happy, pleasant grandchildren who present themselves well, command a certain type of attention; for example, these children might not receive immediate attention because they seem okay when, in fact, special personal care might be needed. Examples of these behaviors are: pleasant, happy, talkative, eager to please, quiet, sad, stoic, and outgoing. Aggressive children many times command direct and sometimes immediate attention from everybody by annoying others and demanding receipt of whatever they want, which is usually everything.

Regardless of the reason for the required attention, grandparents are responsive to and provide care to modify behaviors and satisfy basic needs. Grandparents also help grandchildren understand that many of the things they want are not basic to their survival, such as all the latest and overabundance of clothes, toys, games, and gifts, as well as being like and doing what friends and classmates do. Grandparents respond in ways that help grandchildren learn what they should know to enjoy success and learn what they can do to make their lives productive.

Family Adjustments. Regardless of the particular behaviors grandchildren manifest, grandparents make continuous efforts to adjust (not give in) to their desires, likes and dislikes, personalities, dental and medical care, physical, social, emotional and educational development, as well as religions needs.

One of the major issues in caring for and teaching grandchildren is *conduct development* (learning and demonstrating proper behavior in the home, in school and in the broader community)—*good vs. bad* behavior with emphasis on stressing the *good* and modeling the life skills of concern, regard, responsibility, benevolence, caring, and kindness toward others. (See Education and Life Skills). There can be no limitations; this must be a continuous topic of conversation in the home. Grandparents need to "teach children to use their emotional and social skills to cope with an increasingly complex area of personal, family and societal stresses." (Shapiro 2003). Teach them to think realistically about their lives—everything being age appropriate.

chapter
TWO

MAKING CHOICES

Making choices means thinking about what you want to do—deciding to do things to avoid or lessen negative and enhance positive consequences. Grandparents teach grandchildren the importance of making choices, deciding for themselves the right things to do. While everyone makes mistakes, grandchildren must be assisted to make choices that generate positive outcomes.

Examples:

Choose to be helpful.
Choose to be happy.
Choose to be healthy.
Choose to play by the rules.
Choose to respect yourself and others.
Choose to share.
Choose to do homework and other assignments and
hand them in to the teacher on time.
Choose to be a friend.
Choose to obey rules—home, school, community and societal.

Teaching and Reinforcing Values. Grandparents teach by example. They explain and help grandchildren understand the meaning of values.

They demonstrate pride and self-respect in daily living and interaction—a quality that engenders self-confidence, self-respect and self-motivation.

PRIDE
*If you don't have it, you can't show it.
If you have it, you can't hide.*

-Zora Neal Hurston

Grandchildren observe and emulate the behavior of those they respect and admire. Think about a time when you recognized in your children/grandchildren aspects of your behavior—actions, speech, and body language. Grandchildren consciously emulate the behavior of those charged with caring for them and/or those deemed important to them.

*Whatever we believe about ourselves
and our abilities comes true for us.*
 - **Susan Taylor**

chapter

THREE

SELF-DIRECTION

Medhus (2001) discusses the need to raise children to be self-directed employing these five qualities:

High self-esteem/self-confidence: Children with these qualities understand and accept their limitations and own their skills and abilities. Esteemed, confident children are o.k. knowing they are weak in some areas, and willingly discuss with clarity things they cannot do. They don't give up when activities become a challenge.

Competence: Understanding and manipulating their surroundings are the hallmarks of competent children, which sometimes causes them to be referred to as obstinate, even difficult. They seem fearless, which tends to frighten caregivers—parents, grandparents, friends. Competent children are encouraged to try new things, to challenge their skills and abilities, keeping in mind that failure is part of growth.

Independence: Competent children take on a sense of independence in their thinking, actions and decision making. Their independent thinking tends to get them in trouble with caregivers and other adults. Therefore, they must be *guided* to assist them to do the right thing. Guided discussions and family talks are helpful in leading children in the right direction.

High moral character: This is an attribute that allows children to choose an action or an activity because it is the right thing to do—not how it would make others feel about them. Children with high moral character think about the well-being of others. They are empathetic and offer assistance. They willingly risk ridicule from peers to do or to speak in favor of helping someone else. Their confidence is not shaken when others criticize or disagree with them.

Being an asset within the group: Few children are recognized and appreciated for their *positive efforts* in group activities. Self-directed children assess group dynamics and get involved based on their observations and their feelings about the benefits of belonging. When, and if they choose to become involved, their observations become more focused on the group behavior. Self-directed children will not become a member of a group that dictates the thinking of individual members, because they think for themselves and don't need the group to feel validated as a person. They can speak up when someone is being treated unfairly—bullied, teased, harassed, ridiculed, embarrassed.

Medhus states that children have an ***internal*** and an ***external*** point of control.

Internal point of control: children make choices based on the consequences they have considered internally based on thought and reason.

They think these are the right choices for them to make. They respond to life rather than react to life. These children are self-inspired—inspired by the products of their own reasoning. They accept failure as an opportunity to grow.

External point of control: Children who operate from an external point of control cannot *filter* outside influences through the process of reason. Their need for approval and acceptance clouds and shapes their choices. They develop a social mask... and operate based on what they assume others want them to be... externally directed children never learn to develop self-talk and self-monitoring skills.

chapter FOUR

HEALTH

Health. Providing for and maintaining grandchildren's health is a continuous process—physically, mentally and certainly financially. If the children came into your care from infancy to three years of age, medical attention would have included all the baby healthcare doctor visits and follow up. If previous medical interventions had not been met, grandparents experience the reality of added medical expenses (to play catch up). It is a blessing if the children are in good health. Handling medical and dental, educational, social issues, and recreational activities tied to finances can sometimes be extremely stressful and challenging even when grandparents are financially and physically able to handle such obligations. For grandparents who are unable to handle on-going finances, there are a number of agencies—local, state, federal and foundations—that provide financial and other types of support. (AARP.org has a GrandCare Toolkit that includes an extensive list of Resources for Grandparents Raising Children). Grandparents move beyond the worry about and the questions of "Why?" "When?" "How?" "What happened?" These only add to the stresses inherent in the grandparenting menu. Questions will soon turn into statements such as: "We don't know what we would do if we didn't have them." "We are so lucky; they bring so much love and joy into our lives."

Grandparents' Physical and Mental Health. Make and use ample time to maintain your health, grandma and grandpa. Plan a time during the day to rest. When the grandchildren are in school, set aside an hour or so each day to enjoy a little quiet time. If they are home, have everyone use quiet time to rest. Nothing but quiet! Seek medical attention often enough to stay on top of your general health. "Stress can take its toll, so be diligent with your own health needs. Don't feel guilty if you need to hire a sitter and take breaks away from home. Be sure to get plenty of sleep." (Carson, 2009).

"Although the number of grandmothers raising grandchildren has grown, there remains a dearth of information about the ways in which these responsibilities affect the psychological well-being of these women." (Pruchno & McKenney). As grandchildren become older, they can assume age-appropriate responsibilities and grandparents can put more emphasis on guiding their lives, which reduces physical and mental energy. As grandchildren continue to grow and develop, they can take on household chores, which generate personal growth in independence. (But, that's another book).

chapter
FIVE

EDUCATION

At this point in life when the grandchildren are in school learning a great deal of what they need to know for the rest of their lives, grandparents' *education* continues as well. Most school curricula include life skills or character education.

The following **Life skills** from Integrated Thematic Instruction (ITI) developed by Susan Kovalik, which are included in some elementary school instruction, will enhance family education and discussions for *effective* and *affective* growth and development:

> *Caring: To show and feel concern for others*
>
> *Common Sense: To use good judgment; thinking things through*
>
> *Cooperation: To work together toward a common goal or purpose*
>
> *Courage: To act according to one's beliefs*

Curiosity: To investigate and seek understanding; a desire to learn and know about a full range of things

Effort: To do your best

Flexibility: The ability to alter plans when necessary

Friendship: To make and keep a friend through mutual trust and caring

Integrity: To act according to what is right and wrong

Initiative: To do something because it needs to be done

Organization: To work, plan, arrange and implement in an orderly way

Patience: To wait calmly for something or someone

Perseverance: To continue in spite of difficulties; to keep at it

Pride: To feel satisfaction from doing your personal best

Problem Solving: To seek solutions

Resourcefulness: To respond to challenges and opportunities in creative ways

Use the Internet to access additional information on life skills for elementary, middle and high school grandchildren.

The knowledge employed in grandparents is quite different from what is required to raise grandchildren in today's society. The knowledge and informational changes are evident because you are older, things have changed, and grandchildren are smarter. They have much more exposure to advanced educational knowledge and activities at an earlier age. *An article in Parenting and Child Health (Internet 2009)*, states that "Children's behavior, their knowledge, their skills, with technology and their language may seem so advanced." They interact, negotiate and navigate the maze of activities in their daily lives effectively with guidance and assistance.

Grandparents are now among the elite living with grandchildren who think they know "everything"—all the questions and all the answers. It is an absolute joy to watch them grow and learn and explain the workings of the world, as they see them, employing various gestures and expressions to emphasize their intentions.

Children, in general, are studying and learning a greater volume of materials across the school curriculum than ever before. Class work and homework are more challenging. Students, however, who are taught by dedicated, energetic, well-trained professionals, and who receive assistance and support at home are successful throughout their educational experiences. There are differences among educators and parents about the amount of information that should be presented at different grade levels.

The curricula are even more challenging at schools in some communities. State mandates and expanding curricula demand cooperative efforts between the home and the school. Children's performance and achievement increase when there are positive efforts between the home and the school.

chapter

SIX

SCHOOL INVOLVEMENT

Grandparents must confer with teachers to plan their school involvement in the following areas:

Curriculum: appropriate to grandchildren's educational needs

Homework: too much, too little, challenge

Teacher and grandparent expectations: understand grandchildren's performance, abilities

Solidify your expectations: confer with teacher(s) on what is expected and agree on follow up assessment

Reactions to and assisting with academic, personal-social, emotional and behavioral issues: Discuss these issues with teachers during conferences; set date and time to follow up

Direct involvement—time commitment (classroom, work at home, PTA and/or school-wide activities): sign up for involvement activities at the beginning of the school year

Following discussion on possible tasks and times they might devote to volunteering, grandparents should make some *definite decisions for themselves regarding the amount of time they will be able to devote,* because running the house and taking care of family require considerable time and effort, which, if overdone, can take an enormous toll on health and family relationships.

chapter
SEVEN

CHILDREN'S HOME LIBRARY

Depending on the age of the grandchildren, grandparents begin with a small book case, which grows into one or two larger cases. As the grandchildren move to higher grade levels, books and book cases typically grow as well. After several years of buying from book stores, Scholastic (school book sales), and gifts from friends and relatives the house begins to shrink. It is time to discuss with the grandchildren the need to share books from time to time to make room for new books. Allow individuals to choose the books they will share.

Home Transformation: It is virtuous to be able to accept change with a positive attitude. You can't wait to shop for new things—clothing, books, toys, games, room decorations, gift items, to name a few. You will soon notice the transformation of your home. The house that used to have mobility continues to shrink.

These acquisitions are sometimes the result of grandparents wanting to give rather than grandchildren wanting to receive. Periodic clearing is necessary; it might be a good idea to hold off on buying until some things are cleared out. Donating usable, clean items to various organizations is an effective way of teaching grandchildren about sharing.

chapter EIGHT

TECHNOLOGY KIDS

For grandparents who are not computer experts and whose grandchildren are some years younger (between 45-60 years younger), their emotional, physical, and mental energy will be raised a notch or two. If grandparents realize that the extent of the grandchildren's computer skills and knowledge is greater than theirs, they begin to wonder if it's time to take on still another task of at least trying to learn as much as grandchildren know. Of course, grandparents will be adding another dimension to the mounds of physical and mental things already on the grandparenting menu.

The most astute computer users among the grandchildren are usually good readers and are the most at ease on the computer. They read everything about locating and downloading information they want to view, or games they want to play, because they are serious about uninterrupted use and malfunctions.

chapter
NINE

RELIGIOUS AND/OR SPIRITUAL GUIDANCE

Throughout history, most children have been raised with some form of religious or spiritual guidance. Grandparents currently raising grandchildren want the help of a higher power in providing guidance and universal rules by which to raise their grandchildren. Spiritual or religious guidance is practiced in various ways.

Family: Keeping in Touch. It is important to stay in touch with family (if the situation permits)—the children's natural parents, other grandparents, siblings, and relatives—to give the grandchildren a sense of connectedness and belonging. Children need to feel that they are part of, and be able to discuss extended family when they engage in activities and discussions with friends and classmates.

Grandchildren need to be able to respond appropriately to questions and statements such as "Why don't you live with your mom and dad?" "How come you live with your grandma and grandpa?" While many adults know that millions of grandparents are raising grandchildren, most children do not.

chapter
TEN

SOCIAL ACTIVITIES

Play dates, family gatherings, visits, reunions, vacations, attending various games, participating in sports at school or in the community, religious and dramatic activities, help to solidify grandchildren's sense of belonging. Minimize associations with family and others who do nothing to enhance the grandchildren's quality of lives—tangibly or intangibly.

Play Dates: Grandchildren benefit from positive interactions with other children—sharing ideas, experiences and discovering the richness of human differences.

Family Gatherings: Grandchildren enjoy meeting family members. They learn about extended family members. They learn about their Connectedness to people they don't see on a daily or regular basis. They observe social interactions, relationships and behaviors.

Visitations: Visiting family members and/or friends give grandchildren the chance to practice the social skills learned at home. They also observe and compare the differences and likenesses of their home environment.

Reunions: This type of family event permits grandchildren to meet the larger, extended family group—babies to seniors—some of whom they have not met, and to enjoy the chance to get acquainted with others.

Vacations: Grandchildren can be instrumental in planning vacations when permitted to assist with vacation decision-making. This engages the family in vacation planning. Engage grandchildren in discussions as follows: funds for the vacation, the type of vacation travel—land, air, water, length of time, and whether they will have responsibilities for vacation activities. Depending on their ages, grandchildren can research various types of family vacations and report findings to the family for discussion and/or approval.

Attending Various Museums, Theatres, Theme Parks: Grandchildren will acquire education, pleasure, excitement, and various positive, mental and emotional experiences from visitations to these children-friendly places. Grandparents will be reminded of their youth experiences.

chapter

ELEVEN

YOUTH ACTIVITIES

There are a number of activities in which grandchildren might be interested that are available in schools and in some communities, some of which are the following: swimming, soccer, softball, baseball, tennis, cheerleading, martial arts, dance (ballet, hip-hop, jazz), community volunteer services, music (instrumental and voice), and theatre (drama and/or comedy). Some children begin to show interest in certain activities as early as four years of age. Keep in mind that for every activity in which you enroll your grandchildren, you enroll yourselves also. Regardless of the activity, grandparents are personally, directly involved. Most community activities, today, require some type of financial responsibility. School activities are less likely to require financial obligations.

chapter

TWELVE

FAMILY HISTORY

Talk to grandchildren about family history. Provide information appropriate for their ages. Care should be taken to give only as much information as comprehensible at a particular a point in time. Be honest when discussing family history. On the topic of "What Grandparents Can Do for Grandchildren," the publication, *Grandparenting* (Internet September 2009), states:

"Keep the family history alive. Help grandchildren to know where they fit in the world by telling stories about the family history. Tell them stories about their parents when they are young. Keep family networks alive. Keep in touch with family members."

Discuss what you know. Research for future discussions, questions about which you have little or no information. Sincere care should be taken to avoid giving information that serves no purpose. It is imperative that grandparents and caregivers keep in mind that the reasons they are doing this most important JOB *(it is truly a job)* is to promote healthy happy lives.

chapter

THIRTEEN

THE JOB

Nurturing: Fostering the life skills and teaching grandchildren to respond to issues in a manner that enhances their lives.

Listening: Responding to grandchildren in a manner that assures them that they are being heard, and that your feedback is appropriate to questions and statements.

Encouraging: Instilling confidence and courage. Helping grandchildren use their abilities and strengths to prepare themselves to work more efficiently and effectively. Creating mental and physical environments that build and enhance their desires to take chances and stretch their minds and talents.

Supporting: Assisting grandchildren in their efforts to live up to their qualifications, objectives, potentials and giving praise for good efforts.

Disciplining—Driving vs. Guiding: Most people teach as they were taught. Grandparents are mindful of their parenting style. It is sometimes necessary to modify the way discipline is administered.

The following are among the more healthy method of disciplining:

1. Setting age-appropriate, clearly defined guidelines and family rules. (The rules will be reinforced many, many times).

2. Engaging children in discussions—questions, answers, and input—that promote understanding, thought and reflection.

3. Following up on and providing reminders when these rules are broken (and they will be) gives grandchildren continued guidance and direction.

4. Exercise appropriate consequences for violations.

References

Carson, Shirley A. "Parenting Grandchildren: The unexpected joys and challenges that come with raising grandkids." http://www.focusonthefamily.com/focusmagazine/parentfamily/A000001275.cfm

Davis, Mary Ellen. <u>Standards-Based Counseling in The Middle School.</u> Bloomington, IN: First Books Library. Author House 2002.

Medhus, Elisa, M.D. <u>Raising Children Who Think for Themselves.</u> New York: MJF Books. 2001.

GrandCare Toolkit. "Resources for Grandparents Raising Children." www.AARP.Org.

Parenting and Child Health: "Grandparenting." Children, Youth and Health Service. http://www.cyh.com/HealthTopics/HealthDetails.aspx?p=ll4&np=99&id=1713

Kovalik, Susan. Integrated Thematic Instruction (ITI). www.journeytoexcellence.org/practice/instruction/theories/iti

Parenting Grandchildren. Oregon State University Extension Family and Community Development http://extension.oregonstate.edu-sufcd/parentchild/grandchildren/index ph

Pruchno, Rachel and McKenney, Dorothy. "The Psychological Well-being of Black and White Grandmothers Raising Grandchildren." The Journal of Gerontology. https://psychsoc.gerontologyjournals.org/cgi/content/full/57/5/P444/

Shapiro, Lawrence E. Ph.D. (2003). How to Raise a Child with a High EQ Emotional Quotient: A Parent's Guide to Emotional Intelligence. New York: Quill. 2003.